This Journal
belongs to:

_____

**Journal
Sumo**

Delicious Recipes for Ageless Skin?

Try these 10 recipe cookbooks at Amazon.

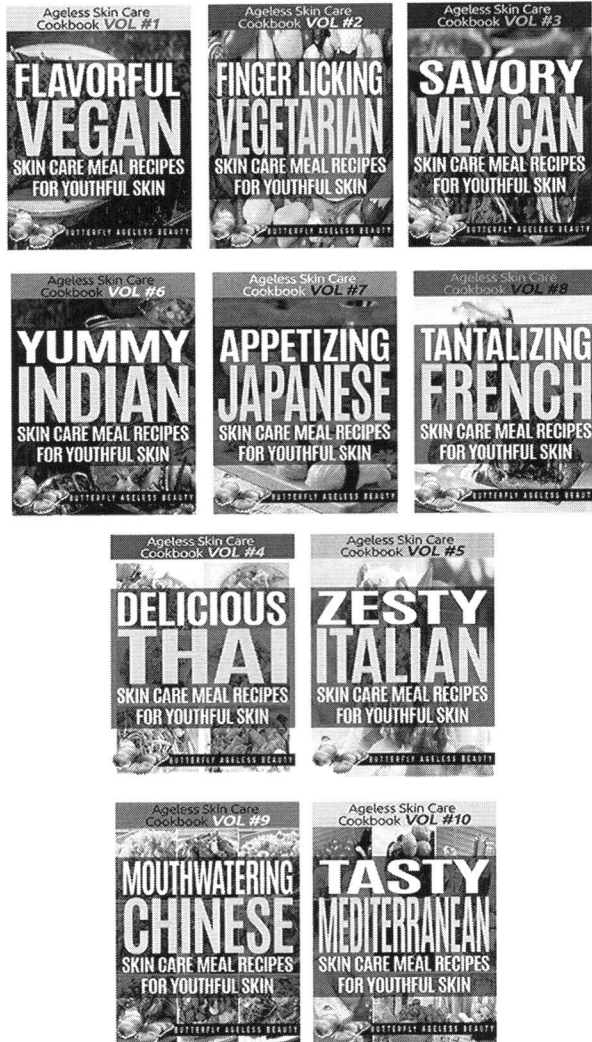

https://amazon.com/author/butterflyagelessbeauty

Journal Writing Prompts

Write about the Past

- Write a letter to your older self.
- Write about your childhood.
- Write about lost friendships.
- Write about regrets you may have.

Write about Yourself

- What frightens you?
- What brings you joy?
- What makes you sad?

Write about the Future

- Where do you want to be 5, 10, or 15 years from now?
- Write down how you can improve your life.
- Write about places you wish to see, vacations you plan to have.
- Write about home improvements you would like to make.

Write about the Present

- Write letters to friends and family members about things you can't say to them in person.
- Write letters to your boss or coworkers.
- Write about your job, pets, your home, etc.
- Write about your daily activities so you can look back and remember each moment.
- Add photos to your entries to make them more special.

My Journal

DATE

PLACE

Write a letter to yourself, or to someone you know.
Put on this paper your daily experiences and feelings.

My Journal

DATE

PLACE

Write a letter to yourself, or to someone you know.
Put on this paper your daily experiences and feelings.

My Journal

DATE

PLACE

Write a letter to yourself, or to someone you know.
Put on this paper your daily experiences and feelings.

My Journal

DATE

PLACE

Write a letter to yourself, or to someone you know.
Put on this paper your daily experiences and feelings.

My Journal

DATE

PLACE

Write a letter to yourself, or to someone you know.
Put on this paper your daily experiences and feelings.

My Journal

DATE

PLACE

Write a letter to yourself, or to someone you know.
Put on this paper your daily experiences and feelings.

_____
_____
_____
_____
_____
_____
_____
_____
_____
_____
_____
_____
_____
_____
_____
_____
_____
_____
_____
_____
_____

My Journal

DATE

PLACE

Write a letter to yourself, or to someone you know.
Put on this paper your daily experiences and feelings.

My Journal

DATE

PLACE

Write a letter to yourself, or to someone you know.
Put on this paper your daily experiences and feelings.

My Journal

DATE

PLACE

Write a letter to yourself, or to someone you know.
Put on this paper your daily experiences and feelings.

My Journal

DATE

PLACE

Write a letter to yourself, or to someone you know.
Put on this paper your daily experiences and feelings.

_____
_____
_____
_____
_____
_____
_____
_____
_____
_____
_____
_____
_____
_____
_____
_____
_____
_____
_____

My Journal

DATE

PLACE

Write a letter to yourself, or to someone you know.
Put on this paper your daily experiences and feelings.

My Journal

DATE

PLACE

Write a letter to yourself, or to someone you know.
Put on this paper your daily experiences and feelings.

My Journal

DATE

PLACE

Write a letter to yourself, or to someone you know.
Put on this paper your daily experiences and feelings.

My Journal

DATE

PLACE

Write a letter to yourself, or to someone you know.
Put on this paper your daily experiences and feelings.

_____

_____

_____

_____

_____

_____

_____

_____

_____

_____

_____

_____

_____

_____

_____

_____

_____

_____

My Journal

DATE

PLACE

Write a letter to yourself, or to someone you know.
Put on this paper your daily experiences and feelings.

My Journal

DATE

PLACE

Write a letter to yourself, or to someone you know.
Put on this paper your daily experiences and feelings.

_____

_____

_____

_____

_____

_____

_____

_____

_____

_____

_____

_____

_____

_____

_____

_____

_____

_____

My Journal

DATE

PLACE

Write a letter to yourself, or to someone you know.
Put on this paper your daily experiences and feelings.

My Journal

DATE

PLACE

Write a letter to yourself, or to someone you know.
Put on this paper your daily experiences and feelings.

_____
_____
_____
_____
_____
_____
_____
_____
_____
_____
_____
_____
_____
_____
_____
_____
_____
_____
_____
_____

My Journal

DATE

PLACE

Write a letter to yourself, or to someone you know.
Put on this paper your daily experiences and feelings.

My Journal

DATE

PLACE

Write a letter to yourself, or to someone you know.
Put on this paper your daily experiences and feelings.

My Journal

DATE

PLACE

Write a letter to yourself, or to someone you know.
Put on this paper your daily experiences and feelings.

My Journal

DATE

PLACE

Write a letter to yourself, or to someone you know.
Put on this paper your daily experiences and feelings.

My Journal

DATE

PLACE

Write a letter to yourself, or to someone you know.
Put on this paper your daily experiences and feelings.

My Journal

DATE

PLACE

Write a letter to yourself, or to someone you know.
Put on this paper your daily experiences and feelings.

My Journal

DATE

PLACE

Write a letter to yourself, or to someone you know.
Put on this paper your daily experiences and feelings.

My Journal

DATE

PLACE

Write a letter to yourself, or to someone you know.
Put on this paper your daily experiences and feelings.

My Journal

DATE

PLACE

Write a letter to yourself, or to someone you know.
Put on this paper your daily experiences and feelings.

My Journal

DATE

PLACE

Write a letter to yourself, or to someone you know.
Put on this paper your daily experiences and feelings.

My Journal

DATE

PLACE

Write a letter to yourself, or to someone you know.
Put on this paper your daily experiences and feelings.

My Journal

DATE

PLACE

Write a letter to yourself, or to someone you know.
Put on this paper your daily experiences and feelings.

My Journal

DATE

PLACE

Write a letter to yourself, or to someone you know.
Put on this paper your daily experiences and feelings.

My Journal

DATE

PLACE

Write a letter to yourself, or to someone you know.
Put on this paper your daily experiences and feelings.

_____

_____

_____

_____

_____

_____

_____

_____

_____

_____

_____

_____

_____

_____

_____

_____

_____

My Journal

DATE

PLACE

Write a letter to yourself, or to someone you know.
Put on this paper your daily experiences and feelings.

_____

_____

_____

_____

_____

_____

_____

_____

_____

_____

_____

_____

_____

_____

_____

_____

_____

_____

_____

My Journal

DATE

PLACE

Write a letter to yourself, or to someone you know.
Put on this paper your daily experiences and feelings.

My Journal

DATE

PLACE

Write a letter to yourself, or to someone you know.
Put on this paper your daily experiences and feelings.

My Journal

DATE

PLACE

Write a letter to yourself, or to someone you know.
Put on this paper your daily experiences and feelings.

My Journal

DATE

PLACE

Write a letter to yourself, or to someone you know.
Put on this paper your daily experiences and feelings.

My Journal

DATE

PLACE

Write a letter to yourself, or to someone you know.
Put on this paper your daily experiences and feelings.

My Journal

DATE

PLACE

Write a letter to yourself, or to someone you know.
Put on this paper your daily experiences and feelings.

My Journal

DATE

PLACE

Write a letter to yourself, or to someone you know.
Put on this paper your daily experiences and feelings.

_____

_____

_____

_____

_____

_____

_____

_____

_____

_____

_____

_____

_____

_____

_____

_____

_____

_____

_____

My Journal

DATE

PLACE

Write a letter to yourself, or to someone you know.
Put on this paper your daily experiences and feelings.

My Journal

DATE

PLACE

Write a letter to yourself, or to someone you know.
Put on this paper your daily experiences and feelings.

_____

_____

_____

_____

_____

_____

_____

_____

_____

_____

_____

_____

_____

_____

_____

_____

_____

_____

My Journal

DATE

PLACE

Write a letter to yourself, or to someone you know.
Put on this paper your daily experiences and feelings.

My Journal

DATE

PLACE

Write a letter to yourself, or to someone you know.
Put on this paper your daily experiences and feelings.

_____

_____

_____

_____

_____

_____

_____

_____

_____

_____

_____

_____

_____

_____

_____

_____

_____

_____

_____

_____

_____

_____

My Journal

DATE

PLACE

Write a letter to yourself, or to someone you know.
Put on this paper your daily experiences and feelings.

My Journal

DATE

PLACE

Write a letter to yourself, or to someone you know.
Put on this paper your daily experiences and feelings.

_____

_____

_____

_____

_____

_____

_____

_____

_____

_____

_____

_____

_____

_____

_____

_____

_____

_____

My Journal

DATE

PLACE

Write a letter to yourself, or to someone you know.
Put on this paper your daily experiences and feelings.

My Journal

DATE

PLACE

Write a letter to yourself, or to someone you know.
Put on this paper your daily experiences and feelings.

My Journal

DATE

PLACE

Write a letter to yourself, or to someone you know.
Put on this paper your daily experiences and feelings.

My Journal

DATE

PLACE

Write a letter to yourself, or to someone you know.
Put on this paper your daily experiences and feelings.

My Journal

DATE

PLACE

Write a letter to yourself, or to someone you know.
Put on this paper your daily experiences and feelings.

My Journal

DATE

PLACE

Write a letter to yourself, or to someone you know.
Put on this paper your daily experiences and feelings.

_____

_____

_____

_____

_____

_____

_____

_____

_____

_____

_____

_____

_____

_____

_____

_____

_____

_____

_____

My Journal

DATE

PLACE

Write a letter to yourself, or to someone you know.
Put on this paper your daily experiences and feelings.

My Journal

DATE

PLACE

Write a letter to yourself, or to someone you know.
Put on this paper your daily experiences and feelings.

My Journal

DATE

PLACE

Write a letter to yourself, or to someone you know.
Put on this paper your daily experiences and feelings.

My Journal

DATE

PLACE

Write a letter to yourself, or to someone you know.
Put on this paper your daily experiences and feelings.

My Journal

DATE

PLACE

Write a letter to yourself, or to someone you know.
Put on this paper your daily experiences and feelings.

_____
_____
_____
_____
_____
_____
_____
_____
_____
_____
_____
_____
_____
_____
_____
_____
_____
_____
_____

My Journal

DATE

PLACE

Write a letter to yourself, or to someone you know.
Put on this paper your daily experiences and feelings.

_____

_____

_____

_____

_____

_____

_____

_____

_____

_____

_____

_____

_____

_____

_____

_____

_____

_____

_____

My Journal

DATE

PLACE

Write a letter to yourself, or to someone you know.
Put on this paper your daily experiences and feelings.

My Journal

DATE

PLACE

Write a letter to yourself, or to someone you know.
Put on this paper your daily experiences and feelings.

My Journal

DATE

PLACE

Write a letter to yourself, or to someone you know.
Put on this paper your daily experiences and feelings.

My Journal

DATE

PLACE

Write a letter to yourself, or to someone you know.
Put on this paper your daily experiences and feelings.

My Journal

DATE

PLACE

Write a letter to yourself, or to someone you know.
Put on this paper your daily experiences and feelings.

My Journal

DATE

PLACE

Write a letter to yourself, or to someone you know.
Put on this paper your daily experiences and feelings.

My Journal

DATE

PLACE

Write a letter to yourself, or to someone you know.
Put on this paper your daily experiences and feelings.

My Journal

DATE

PLACE

Write a letter to yourself, or to someone you know.
Put on this paper your daily experiences and feelings.

My Journal

DATE

PLACE

Write a letter to yourself, or to someone you know.
Put on this paper your daily experiences and feelings.

My Journal

DATE

PLACE

Write a letter to yourself, or to someone you know.
Put on this paper your daily experiences and feelings.

_____

_____

_____

_____

_____

_____

_____

_____

_____

_____

_____

_____

_____

_____

_____

_____

_____

_____

_____

My Journal

DATE

PLACE

Write a letter to yourself, or to someone you know.
Put on this paper your daily experiences and feelings.

My Journal

DATE

PLACE

Write a letter to yourself, or to someone you know.
Put on this paper your daily experiences and feelings.

My Journal

DATE

PLACE

Write a letter to yourself, or to someone you know.
Put on this paper your daily experiences and feelings.

My Journal

DATE

PLACE

Write a letter to yourself, or to someone you know.
Put on this paper your daily experiences and feelings.

My Journal

DATE

PLACE

Write a letter to yourself, or to someone you know.
Put on this paper your daily experiences and feelings.

My Journal

DATE

PLACE

Write a letter to yourself, or to someone you know.
Put on this paper your daily experiences and feelings.

My Journal

DATE

PLACE

Write a letter to yourself, or to someone you know.
Put on this paper your daily experiences and feelings.

My Journal

DATE

PLACE

Write a letter to yourself, or to someone you know.
Put on this paper your daily experiences and feelings.

My Journal

DATE

PLACE

Write a letter to yourself, or to someone you know.
Put on this paper your daily experiences and feelings.

My Journal

DATE

PLACE

Write a letter to yourself, or to someone you know.
Put on this paper your daily experiences and feelings.

My Journal

DATE

PLACE

Write a letter to yourself, or to someone you know.
Put on this paper your daily experiences and feelings.

My Journal

DATE

PLACE

Write a letter to yourself, or to someone you know.
Put on this paper your daily experiences and feelings.

My Journal

DATE

PLACE

Write a letter to yourself, or to someone you know.
Put on this paper your daily experiences and feelings.

My Journal

DATE

PLACE

Write a letter to yourself, or to someone you know.
Put on this paper your daily experiences and feelings.

_____
_____
_____
_____
_____
_____
_____
_____
_____
_____
_____
_____
_____
_____
_____
_____
_____
_____
_____
_____

My Journal

DATE

PLACE

Write a letter to yourself, or to someone you know.
Put on this paper your daily experiences and feelings.

_____

_____

_____

_____

_____

_____

_____

_____

_____

_____

_____

_____

_____

_____

_____

_____

_____

_____

_____

My Journal

DATE

PLACE

Write a letter to yourself, or to someone you know.
Put on this paper your daily experiences and feelings.

_____

_____

_____

_____

_____

_____

_____

_____

_____

_____

_____

_____

_____

_____

_____

_____

_____

_____

_____

_____

_____

_____

My Journal

DATE

PLACE

Write a letter to yourself, or to someone you know.
Put on this paper your daily experiences and feelings.

My Journal

DATE

PLACE

Write a letter to yourself, or to someone you know.
Put on this paper your daily experiences and feelings.

My Journal

DATE

PLACE

Write a letter to yourself, or to someone you know.
Put on this paper your daily experiences and feelings.

My Journal

DATE

PLACE

Write a letter to yourself, or to someone you know.
Put on this paper your daily experiences and feelings.

My Journal

Write a letter to yourself, or to someone you know.
Put on this paper your daily experiences and feelings.

My Journal

DATE

PLACE

Write a letter to yourself, or to someone you know.
Put on this paper your daily experiences and feelings.

_____

_____

_____

_____

_____

_____

_____

_____

_____

_____

_____

_____

_____

_____

_____

_____

_____

_____

_____

_____

My Journal

DATE

PLACE

Write a letter to yourself, or to someone you know.
Put on this paper your daily experiences and feelings.

_____

_____

_____

_____

_____

_____

_____

_____

_____

_____

_____

_____

_____

_____

_____

_____

_____

_____

_____

My Journal

DATE

PLACE

Write a letter to yourself, or to someone you know.
Put on this paper your daily experiences and feelings.

My Journal

DATE

PLACE

Write a letter to yourself, or to someone you know.
Put on this paper your daily experiences and feelings.

My Journal

DATE

PLACE

Write a letter to yourself, or to someone you know.
Put on this paper your daily experiences and feelings.

My Journal

DATE

PLACE

Write a letter to yourself, or to someone you know.
Put on this paper your daily experiences and feelings.

My Journal

DATE

PLACE

Write a letter to yourself, or to someone you know.
Put on this paper your daily experiences and feelings.

My Journal

DATE

PLACE

Write a letter to yourself, or to someone you know.
Put on this paper your daily experiences and feelings.

My Journal

DATE

PLACE

Write a letter to yourself, or to someone you know.
Put on this paper your daily experiences and feelings.

My Journal

DATE

PLACE

Write a letter to yourself, or to someone you know.
Put on this paper your daily experiences and feelings.

My Journal

DATE

PLACE

Write a letter to yourself, or to someone you know.
Put on this paper your daily experiences and feelings.

_____

_____

_____

_____

_____

_____

_____

_____

_____

_____

_____

_____

_____

_____

_____

_____

_____

_____

_____

Printed in Great
Britain
by Amazon

32424650R00059